A PRIMARY SOURCE HISTORY
OF THE UNITED STATES

THE CRISIS OF THE UNION

1815–1865

George E. Stanley

WORLD ALMANAC® LIBRARY

Please visit our web site at: www.worldalmanaclibrary.com
For a free color catalog describing World Almanac® Library's list of high-quality
books and multimedia programs, call 1-800-848-2928 (USA) or 1-800-387-3178
(Canada). World Almanac® Library's fax: (414) 332-3567.

Library of Congress Cataloging-in-Publication Data available upon request from publisher.
Fax (414) 336-0157 for the attention of the Publishing Records Department.

ISBN 0-8368-5826-3 (lib. bdg.)
ISBN 0-8368-5835-2 (softcover)

First published in 2005 by
World Almanac® Library
330 West Olive Street, Suite 100
Milwaukee, WI 53212 USA

Produced by Byron Preiss Visual Publications Inc.
Project Editor: Susan Hoe
Designer: Marisa Gentile
World Almanac® Library editor: Alan Wachtel
World Almanac® Library art direction: Tammy West

Picture acknowledgements:
Library of Congress: Cover (lower left and lower right), pp. 4, 8, 9, 11, 13, 15, 17, 18, 20, 23,
24, 27 (upper left), 27 (lower right), 29, 31, 33, 35, 37, 38, 39, 40, 42, 43; National Archives:
pp. 5, 7; The Granger Collection, New York: Cover (upper left and upper right), pp. 19, 21

Printed in the United States of America

1 2 3 4 5 6 7 8 9 09 08 07 06 05

Dr. George E. Stanley is a professor at Cameron University in Lawton, Oklahoma. He has authored
more than eighty books for young readers, many in the field of history and science. Dr. Stanley recently
completed a series of history books on famous Americans, including *Geronimo, Andrew Jackson,
Harry S. Truman,* and *Mr. Rogers.*

CONTENTS

Through the examination of authentic historical documents, including charters, diaries, journals, letters, speeches, and other written records, each title in *A Primary Source History of the United States* offers a unique perspective on the events that shaped the United States. In addition to providing important historical information, each document serves as a piece of living history that opens a window into the kinds of thinking and modes of expression that characterized the various epochs of American history.

Note: To facilitate the reading of older documents, the modern-day spelling of certain words is used.

CHAPTER 1

Nationalism

1815–1824

Nationalism surged after the War of 1812, and this new spirit encouraged the economy and promoted western expansion at home, trade abroad, and assertiveness throughout the Western Hemisphere. This new self-confidence among Americans was encouraged by the Democratic-Republicans who borrowed a page from what was usually the Federalists' agenda.

Americans were still angry about the Hartford Convention and New England's opposition to the war, so in 1816, the voters completely rejected the Federalist party, destroying it as a political force in American politics, and elected James Monroe, a Virginia Democratic-Republican, as president. For a few years, until other political parties formed, there was almost no formal opposition to Monroe's policies.

PRESIDENT MONROE'S FIRST INAUGURAL ADDRESS: 1817

▲ James Monroe was the fifth U.S. president.

Washington, March 4, 1817

… Such … is the … Government under which we live—a Government adequate to every purpose for which the social compact is formed; a Government elective in all its branches, under which every citizen may by his merit obtain the highest trust by the Constitution; which contains within it no cause of discord, none to put … one portion of the community with another; a Government which protects every citizen … of his rights, and is able to protect the nation against injustice from foreign powers….

THE ERA OF GOOD FEELING

Monroe's presidency was known as the "Era of Good Feeling." The Embargo Act, which had forbidden all exports from the United States to any country, had been repealed. The country was at peace, and the president sought a reconciliation of political differences. Still, divisive political issues surfaced.

The Supreme Court began handing down decisions that clearly favored a strong national government. In a case involving Dartmouth College, the Supreme Court ruled that state charters granted to private organizations were protected by the Constitution and that state legislatures could not change them.

In the case of *McCulloch* v. *Maryland,* the Supreme Court denied states the power to tax a federal agency—in this particular instance, the Second Bank of the United States. Chief Justice John Marshall felt that while the powers of the federal government were limited, the government was supreme within its sphere of action.

McCulloch v. *Maryland* Opinion: 1819

… It being the opinion of the Court that the act incorporating the bank [of the United States] is constitutional; and that the power of establishing a branch in the State of Maryland might be properly exercised by the bank itself, we proceed to inquire whether the State of Maryland may, without violating the Constitution, tax that branch.…

We are unanimously of the opinion, that the law passed by the legislature of Maryland, imposing a tax on the Bank of the United States, is unconstitutional and void.…

This handwritten *McCulloch* v. *Maryland* decision denied the states the power to tax a federal agency. ▶

SLAVE STATES AND FREE STATES

Although nationalism brought the country together, slavery separated it. In fact, with the exception of an act ending the foreign slave trade after January 1, 1808—which passed Congress without much opposition—the nation's political leaders had tried to avoid dealing with the issue of slavery ever since the Constitution was drafted. The moral questions that slavery raised made it a difficult topic.

Slavery in the North had almost died out, and most people in that part of the country considered it evil. Southerners, on the other hand, wanted slaves to work the vast plantations. They accused Northern abolitionists of trying to destroy the Union.

In 1819, the Missouri Territory applied for admission into the Union as a slave state, a move that would thrust slavery farther northward if successful. It would also tilt the uneasy political balance in the Senate toward the slave states. Henry Clay of Kentucky helped reach what was called "the Missouri Compromise." He suggested that Maine, which at that time was part of Massachusetts, be admitted as a free state, followed by Missouri's admission as a slave state, thus preserving the balance.

THE MONROE DOCTRINE

James Monroe easily won reelection in 1820 because there was no other political party to challenge him. His only opposition was from his secretary of state, John Quincy Adams, who ran as an independent and received one electoral vote.

In 1822, in an effort to insulate the Western Hemisphere from European conflicts, the United States became the first nation to recognize several new countries in Latin America—including Mexico, which had just won its independence from Spain. Not long after, however, a revolt in Spain forced France to occupy that country. The United States feared that France would try to return the new Latin American countries to Spanish rule. Great Britain suggested a joint U.S.-British declaration against European intervention in the Western Hemisphere, but it was rejected.

In his seventh annual message to Congress, on December 2, 1823, President Monroe established principles of U.S. foreign policy that became known as the Monroe Doctrine and are still adhered to today. The United States will not tolerate the interference of European or Asian nations in the affairs of the Western Hemisphere.

THE MONROE DOCTRINE: 1820

... The occasion has been judged proper for asserting, as a principle in which the rights and the interests of the United States are involved, that the American continents, by the free and independent condition which they have assumed and maintain, are henceforth not to be considered as subjects for future colonization by any European powers....

We should consider any attempt on [Europe's] part to extend their system [of government] to any portion of this hemisphere, as dangerous to our peace and safety....

The Era of Good Feeling did not last Monroe's two terms as president. Because there were no other formal political parties, most of the Federalists had joined the Democratic-Republicans, but they found themselves in disagreement over many issues, especially those dealing with taxes and trade. Eventually, these former Federalists would form a new party—the Whigs.

By 1824, nationalism had been replaced by sectionalism. Instead of seeing the nation as a whole, Americans had decided that local interests—such as pro-slavery and farming in the South and anti-slavery and manufacturing in the North— were more important. Thus, even as major developments in transportation

▲ The Monroe Doctrine was presented at the first session of Congress in 1823 by President James Monroe.

(such as railroads and canals) and in communication and a greater number of post offices around the country worked to unite the nation, political differences threatened to tear it apart.

CHAPTER 2

Government Reforms

1824–1832

In the presidential election of 1824, Andrew Jackson, the hero of the War of 1812, received forty-three percent of the popular vote but not the majority of electoral votes. The top four vote getters, including Jackson, were Secretary of State John Quincy Adams, Secretary of the Treasury William Crawford, and Henry Clay, a senator from Kentucky.

According to the Constitution, members of the House of Representatives had to decide the winner. Clay did not like Jackson, and he was able to convince the other legislators to vote for Adams. Adams, the son of former president John Adams, became the sixth president of the United States. Jackson and his supporters felt the election had been stolen from them.

▲ This 1824 cartoon shows the race for president. Adams, Crawford, and Jackson are near the finish line, while Clay is a distant fourth on the far right.

Even though Adams seemed well qualified for the job, he had a disappointing term in office. He faced opposition everywhere he turned, from Andrew Jackson's backers and from South Carolina Senator John C. Calhoun, who used his influence to fill Senate committees with men who did not support Adams's policies.

PROTECTIVE TARIFFS

One of the most important domestic issues of the time was protective tariffs that imposed duties on many imported goods. Henry Clay advocated a protective tariff to encourage domestic manufacturing while generating money to build harbors and canals. In a two-day-long speech, Clay championed the Tariff of 1824.

▲ An undated print of Henry Clay, who was not only a senator but a slaveholding planter and lawyer from Kentucky.

CLAY'S SPEECH ON THE TARIFF OF 1824: 1824

… And what is this tariff? It seems to have been regarded as a sort of monster, huge and deformed; a wild beast, endowed with tremendous powers of destruction, about to be let loose among our people, if not to devour them, at least to consume their substance. But let us calm our passions, and deliberately survey this alarming, this terrific being. The sole object of the tariff is to tax the produce of foreign industry, with the view of promoting American industry. The tax is exclusively levelled at foreign industry.…

❝The tax is exclusively levelled at foreign industry.…❞

INDIAN LAND CESSIONS

Many Americans believed that the nation's economic growth was tied to land. Through various treaties with the United States, Indian groups had already given up thousands of acres, but the United States government and the white settlers weren't satisfied.

In Georgia, Governor George Troup saw the Creek Indians as a serious problem. They had begun giving up their tribal ways and adopting American culture. Troup believed that white settlers moving west might find it harder to "dispose" of "assimilated" Indians. So, in 1825, Troup, with the blessings of the federal government, manipulated Creek Chief William McIntosh into ceding all Lower Creek land to Georgia in the February 12, 1825, Treaty of Indian Springs.

TREATY OF INDIAN SPRINGS: 1825

… The Creek nation cede to the United States all the lands lying within the boundaries of the State of Georgia….

It is further agreed … that the United States will give, in exchange for the lands hereby acquired, the like quantity, acre for acre, westward of the Mississippi, on the Arkansas river, commencing at the mouth of the Canadian fork thereof, and running westward between the said rivers Arkansas and Canadian fork for quantity….

By agreeing to this treaty, the Creek people felt betrayed by Chief McIntosh, and he was murdered by angry tribe members. Nevertheless, the treaty was ratified by Congress. Governor Troup's stand on Indians made him popular among the settlers in Georgia, and he began to force the Creek from the rest of their lands. President Adams tried to stop him with threats of a military intervention, but Troup called in the Georgia militia. Adams backed down, saying that the Indians were not worth going to war over. By 1827, the Creek were gone from Georgia.

ABOLITIONISTS

Slavery was a serious problem for the writers of the Constitution. It divided the nation from the very beginning. Although some Southerners did see slavery as an evil, they considered it a necessary evil for the good of the agricultural economy of the region. Since slaves were not important to the manufacturing economy of the North, most Northerners simply viewed slavery as an evil institution, although few were willing to do anything about it.

As new states came into the Union, the government tried to keep a balance between free states and slave states. Congress hoped that the Missouri Compromise of 1820 would put the slavery issue to rest. But, in fact, abolitionists—people who wanted an end to slavery—became even more vocal in their attacks.

Moses Elias Levy was one of the few Southerners to propose emancipation—even if he was in the relative safety of London when he made his views public in 1828 in a document entitled "A Plan for the Abolition of Slavery, Consistently with the Interests of All Parties Concerned."

At the Philadelphia Convention in 1787, Southerners, especially planters, wanted slaves to be counted

MOSES LEVY'S ABOLITION PLAN: 1828

… Having devoted my attention to the abolition of Slavery for the last twenty years … [I now suggest that] the emigration of white people to America will not only prove the most effectual method of destroying slavery, and of consolidating the newly-formed government, but Europe itself will be greatly benefitted.… The … black population will be thus neutralized, and, by attending to the education of their freeborn offspring, the now wild wastes of America will be populated by an enlightened generation, in which the black skin will be lost with slavery in the gradual shades of improvement.…

▲ This 1837 woodcut of a slave was used in an anti-slavery publication. It asks the question, "Am I not a man and a brother?"

as part of the population because this would give them more representatives in Congress. Northerners were opposed to this proposal. When Southerners threatened not to join the Union, a compromise was reached. Each slave would be counted as three-fifths of a person.

THE TARIFF OF 1828

Southerners depended more on imports than people in any other part of the country, so the Tariff of 1828, which levied additional tariffs on imported goods, was considered both discriminatory and unconstitutional.

Many Southerners felt that their rights had been sacrificed to meet the demands of northern industrialists. They also feared the act could set a precedent for legislation on slavery. In December 1828, John C. Calhoun responded with a speech that suggested all states should have the right to nullify a law passed by Congress that they considered unjust.

CALHOUN'S SOUTH CAROLINA EXPOSITION AND PROTEST SPEECH: 1828

66 The violation then consists in using a power granted for one object, to advance another.... 99

... [The Federal] Government is one of specific powers, and it can rightfully exercise only the powers expressly granted, and those that may be "necessary and proper" to carry them into effect; all others being reserved expressly to the States, or to the people. It results necessarily, that those who claim to exercise a power under the Constitution, are bound to shew [sic], that it is expressly granted, or that it is necessary and proper, as a means to some of the granted powers. It is true that the [eighth] section of the first article of the Constitution of the United States authorizes Congress to lay and collect an impost duty, but it is granted as a tax power, for the sole purpose of revenue; a power in its nature essentially different from that of imposing protective or prohibitory duties.... The violation then consists in using a power granted for one object, to advance another, and that by the sacrifice of the original object....

ANDREW JACKSON— PRESIDENT OF THE COMMON PEOPLE

The presidential campaign of 1828 was more about the personal backgrounds of the two candidates than it was about the issues. Andrew Jackson denounced Adams for being an "aristocrat." Supporters of Adams called Jackson an "illiterate backwoodsman." But ordinary Americans admired the leadership qualities that Jackson displayed in the Battle of New Orleans during the War of 1812 as well as his decisive dealings with the Indians.

▲ This 1828 painting of Andrew Jackson was issued during his run for the presidency in 1828.

Jackson secured support from the western part of the country. As a slave owner, he could also count on support from the South. Adams's support came only from New England. Most Americans seemed to

PRESIDENT JACKSON'S FIRST INAUGURAL ADDRESS: 1829

… About to undertake the arduous duties that I have been appointed to perform by the choice of a free people, I avail myself of this customary and solemn occasion to express the gratitude which their confidence inspires.…

As the instrument of the Federal Constitution it will devolve on me for a stated period to execute the laws of the United States.…

In administering the laws of Congress I shall keep steadily in view the limitation as well as the extent of the Executive power, trusting thereby to discharge the functions of my office without transcending its authority.…

It will be my sincere and constant desire to observe toward the Indian tribes within our limits a just and liberal policy.…

forget about the important role Adams had played in negotiating the Treaty of Ghent, which ended the War of 1812. Jackson easily won the election.

Even in the White House, Jackson was a fighter. He argued constantly with his advisers, fired many government employees, refused to obey Supreme Court decisions, and took government money away from the Bank of the United States.

Jackson's solution to the Indian land question was to pass The Indian Removal Act of 1830, which directed tribes to be resettled west of the Mississippi River. But when the state of Georgia tried to drive the Cherokees out, they took their case to the Supreme Court. Although Chief Justice John Marshall ruled in favor of the Indians, President Jackson refused to obey the order and in fact challenged Marshall to try to enforce it.

THE INDIAN REMOVAL ACT: 1830

Be it enacted ... [that] it shall be lawful for the President of the United States to cause so much of any territory belonging to the United States, west of the river Mississippi, not included in any state or organized territory, and to which the Indian title has been extinguished, as he may judge necessary, to be divided into a suitable number of districts, for the reception of such tribes or nations of Indians as may choose to exchange the lands where they now reside, and remove there; and to cause each of said districts to be so described by natural or artificial marks, as to be easily distinguished from every other....

SLAVE REVOLTS

Early on the morning of August 22, 1831, Nat Turner, a Virginia slave preacher, led the biggest slave uprising in American history. He and his men began by killing Turner's master and his family in their beds and continued on across the Virginia countryside, killing all of the white people they encountered. As they went from house to house, Turner's force grew to more than forty slaves.

Within hours, an army of white men confronted the rebels, causing them to scatter. The next day Nat Turner and his remaining men were repulsed when the Virginia militia arrived with a force of three thousand men and crushed the uprising. But

NAT TURNER'S CONFESSIONS: 1831

You have asked me to give a history of the motives which induced me to undertake the late insurrection, as you call it. To do so I must go back to the days of my infancy.... In my childhood a circumstance occurred which made an indelible impression on my mind, and laid the groundwork of that enthusiasm, which has terminated so fatally to many, both white and black, and for which I am about to atone at the gallows.... Being at play with other children ... I was telling them something, which my mother overhearing, said it had happened before I was born.... Others being called on were greatly astonished ... and caused them to say in my hearing, I surely would be a prophet....

once again, Nat Turner managed to escape. After six weeks, he was finally captured, tried, and sentenced to death. As he waited to be hanged, Turner talked about the uprising with his lawyer, Thomas R. Gray, and told him how he had come to his "calling."

In the hysteria that followed the uprising, some two hundred blacks in Virginia and North Carolina were killed. The rebellion put an end to whites' belief that slaves were content with their lot and too servile to revolt. New laws were passed to regulate what slaves and free blacks could and could not do. Virginia's legislature passed laws that restricted the movement and assembly of black people, slave or free. Laws also made it illegal to teach slaves to read. Whites intended to make sure that there would be no more insurrections.

◀ This 1831 woodcut shows some scenes from the uprising led by Nat Turner.

15

CHAPTER 3

Economic and Social Reforms

1832–1848

Andrew Jackson hated banks, paper money, and anyone who profited from them, but most of his anger was directed at the Second National Bank of the United States because it was controlled by private citizens and acted as the cred-itor for state banks, which were required to repay their loans in hard currency, not with their own notes.

Established in 1816, the Second Bank was due for a new charter in 1836, but Nicholas Biddle, its president, wanted to get the bank rechartered four years ahead of the expiration date. Despite the fact that Congress passed the necessary legislation by a fairly large margin, President Jackson vetoed the bill, and its supporters did not have enough votes to override the veto. Jackson denounced the early re-chartering scheme and condemned the bank as a privileged monopoly. Although the status of the bank had been upheld by the Supreme Court in *McCulloch* v. *Maryland* in 1819, President Jackson still considered it unconstitutional.

ANDREW JACKSON'S BANK VETO MESSAGE: 1832

… The Bank of the United States … enjoys an exclusive privilege of banking under the authority of the General Government, a monopoly of its favor and support.…

Is there no danger to our liberty and independence in a bank that in its nature has so little to bind it to our country?… It is to be regretted that the rich and powerful too often bend the acts of government to their selfish purposes.…

We can at least take a stand against all new grants of monopolies and exclusive privileges, against … the advancement of a few at the expense of many.…

This 1836 cartoon shows Jackson slaying a many-headed monster—the Bank of the United States. ▶

In 1832, voters again elected Andrew Jackson. But in November of that year, South Carolina passed the Ordinance of Nullification, which said the state had the right to nullify any law passed by Congress. The law they wanted to nullify was the Tariff of 1828, which Southerners opposed because it forbade customs duties from being collected in South Carolina's port cities.

As a counter measure, President Jackson submitted a force bill to Congress that would allow the use of federal troops in South Carolina to enforce the government's laws. He sent a proclamation to the people of the state to support this action.

JACKSON'S PROCLAMATION TO THE PEOPLE OF SOUTH CAROLINA: 1832

… I consider, then, the power to annul a law of the United States, assumed by one state, incompatible with the existence of the Union, contradicted expressly by the letter of the Constitution, unauthorized by its spirit, inconsistent with every principle on which it was founded, and destructive of the great object for which it was formed.…

— ★ —

Unfortunately, Jackson's proclamation evoked a defiant response from the people, but without enough support from the other Southern states, South Carolina was forced to retreat. Eventually, with the help of Henry Clay, a more moderate tariff bill was passed.

EUROPE LOOKS AT AMERICAN DEMOCRACY

Alexis de Tocqueville, a French nobleman, spent nine months in the United States between 1831 and 1832 and wrote a study called *Democracy in America*. Published in 1835, Tocqueville's study gave a perceptive analysis of how the forces of democracy and equality had forged every aspect of American life, including the social institutions of family and religion. Tocqueville observed that there was no hereditary noble class and that distinctions in speech, manners, and clothing were far less noticeable than in European countries. Yet he feared that what he called the "tyranny of the majority" would force people to give up their individualism.

ALEXIS DE TOCQUEVILLE'S *DEMOCRACY IN AMERICA*: 1835

... Among the novel objects that attracted my attention during my stay in the United States, nothing struck me more forcibly than the general equality of condition among the people....

The electors see their representative not only as a legislator for the state but also as the natural protector of local interests in the legislature; indeed, they

▲ A 1901 print of Alexis de Tocqueville, a French aristocrat who wrote about his impressions of the United States.

almost seem to think that he has a power of attorney to represent each constituent, and they trust him to be as eager in their private interests as in those of the country....

There is hardly a congressman prepared to go home until he has at least one speech printed and sent to his constituents, and he won't let anybody interrupt his harangue until he had made all of his ... suggestions about the 24 states of the Union, and ... the district he represents....

They [journalists] certainly are not great writers, but they speak their country's language and they make themselves heard....

CONSTITUTION OF THE AMERICAN ANTI-SLAVERY SOCIETY: 1833

... The objects of this Society are the entire abolition of Slavery in the United States. While it admits that each State, in which Slavery exists, had, by the Constitution of the United States, the exclusive right to legislate in regard to its abolition in said State, it shall aim to convince all our fellow-citizens ... that Slaveholding is a heinous crime in the sight of God, and that the duty ... and best interests of all concerned, require its immediate abandonment....

This Society shall aim to elevate the ... condition of the people of color ... but ... will never ... countenance the oppressed ... by resorting to physical force....

SOCIAL REFORMS

During the nineteenth century, various reform movements started to organize into groups. Slavery was still an issue that divided the nation. On December 4, 1833, the American Anti-Slavery Society met in Philadelphia to write its constitution. The Society pledged to end slavery in the United States. The principles adopted at the founding meeting established the basic argument that slavery was illegal— if not under the U.S. Constitution, then certainly under natural law.

In the 1840s, female activists began splitting from the abolitionists and started turning their attention to their own situation. In 1848, Elizabeth Cady Stanton helped organize the first women's rights convention in the United States. In her Seneca Falls Declaration, Stanton stated that "... such has been the patient sufferance of the women under this government, and such is now the necessity which constrains them to demand the equal station to which they are entitled...."

Elizabeth C. Stanton *(left)* and Susan B. Anthony *(right)* were early advocates for women's rights. ▶

CHAPTER 4

Westward Expansion

1824–1848

In the winter of 1824, some Crow Indians showed a small band of fur trappers an easy way to cross the Rocky Mountains. This route eventually became the Oregon Trail and was the main route for settlers heading west in the United States. It stretched from Missouri to Oregon's Willamette Valley. John Ball, a member of an expedition to the Rockies and the Pacific Northwest, wrote an account of his trip entitled "Across the Plains to Oregon and the Return Home by Cape Horn, 1832–1835."

▲ As more people moved west, new settlements, such as the one shown in this lithograph, c.1868, sprang up along the way.

BALL'S ACCOUNT OF HIS TRIP WEST: 1832–1835

… We could not see a buffalo for a day or two, and then in countless number … probably 10,000.…

Indians approached near camp and raised their whoop and fired guns and arrows.… We found in the morning … [they] had stolen some dozen or more of our best horses.…

Five of us took an Indian canoe and paddled down the [Columbia] … there to stand on the brink of the great Pacific, with the rolling waves washing its sands and seaweeds to my feet.…

Texas Independence

In 1821, Mexico won its independence from Spain and inherited all the land from Texas to the Pacific Ocean. American settlers came to Texas by the thousands. Mexico's General Santa Anna tried to tighten his control, but the Texans rebelled. In early 1836, Santa Anna marched several thousand soldiers northward to subdue them. At the Alamo, an abandoned mission in San Antonio, Texas, less than two hundred settlers, under the command of William Barret Travis and including Jim Bowie and Davy Crockett, tried to fight off Santa Anna's force.

WILLIAM BARRET TRAVIS, LETTER FROM THE COMMANDANCY OF THE ALAMO: 1836

Feb. 24th, 1836

To all the People of Texas & all Americans in the World— ...

I am besieged by a thousand or more of the Mexicans under Santa Anna—I have sustained a continual Bombardment & cannonade for 24 hours & have not lost a man.... I call on you ... to come to our aid.... If this call is neglected, I am determined to sustain myself as long as possible & die like a soldier who never forgets what is due to his own honor & that of his country....

P.S. The Lord is on our side— ...

On March 6, the Mexican army overran the Alamo and killed all the defenders, but on April 21, the Texans defeated the Mexican army for good at the Battle of San Jacinto. Texas established the independent Lone Star Republic but soon sought annexation to the United States as a slave state.

▲ A nineteenth century engraving depicts Mexico's General Santa Anna and his troops storming the Alamo.

NEW POLITICAL ALIGNMENTS

Martin Van Buren was elected president in 1836, but an economic crisis soon gripped the nation. By late 1837, more than one third of Americans were out of work and many more were only able to find part-time jobs. Even though Van Buren was blamed for the depression, the Democrats still nominated him for a second term. But the Whig candidate, William Henry Harrison, won the election of 1840.

Right after his inauguration, Harrison died of pneumonia. Vice President John Tyler became president, but he had so many political enemies that he was not able to accomplish much. One of his successful acts in office, however, was to annex Texas on March 1, 1845.

JOINT RESOLUTION TO ANNEX TEXAS: 1845

... Resolved by the Senate and House of Representatives of the United States of America in Congress assembled, That Congress doth consent that the territory properly included within, and rightfully belonging to the Republic of Texas, may be erected into a new state, to be called the state of Texas, with a republican form of government, to be adopted by the people of said republic, by deputies in Convention assembled, with the consent of the existing government, in order that the same may be admitted as one of the states of this Union....

THE RISE OF MANIFEST DESTINY

In 1837, at the age of 23, John L. O'Sullivan, a lawyer and Democratic party activist, founded *The United States Magazine and Democratic Review,* an outlet for his own romantic views on the future of democracy in the United States and a vehicle that he used for Democratic party propaganda.

O'Sullivan was especially obsessed with the notion that the main mission of the United States was to spread democracy across the continent. In an article called "Annexation" in the

July and August 1845 issue of his magazine, he coined the term *Manifest Destiny* to justify westward expansion. O'Sullivan's vision of his country's promise shaped the way in which Americans understood their relationship to neighboring countries and, later, to the entire world.

In 1844, Democrat James K. Polk, an aggressive expansionist, defeated the Whig candidate Henry Clay for the presidency. The Democratic platform called for the entry of Texas into the Union and for the settlement of Oregon, which Great Britain also claimed. American expansion had begun in earnest.

O'SULLIVAN'S ARTICLE ON MANIFEST DESTINY: 1845

... Other nations have undertaken to intrude themselves ... in a spirit of hostile interference against us, for the avowed object of thwarting our policy and hampering our power, limiting our greatness and checking the fulfillment of our manifest destiny to overspread the continent allotted by Providence for the free development of our yearly multiplying millions....

▼ A print, c.1873, depicts Manifest Destiny as an allegorical figure leading pioneers west.

This lithograph, c.1847, depicts General Zachary Taylor at the Battle of Buena Vista during the Mexican War. ▶

WAR WITH MEXICO

Mexico broke off diplomatic relations with the United States when Congress annexed Texas. President Polk sent John Slidell to Mexico with a proposal to purchase New Mexico and California and settle the boundary of Texas at the Rio Grande. In March 1846, however, the Mexican government was overthrown, and the new Mexican president reaffirmed Mexico's claims to all of Texas. President Polk ordered General Zachary Taylor and his troops to the Rio Grande to keep the Mexicans from crossing it.

PRESIDENT POLK'S MESSAGE TO CONGRESS: 1846

... In further vindication of our rights and defense of [Texas], I involve the prompt action of Congress to recognize the existence of the war [with Mexico], and to place at the disposition of the Executive the means of prosecuting the war with vigor, and thus hastening the restoration of peace. To this end I recommend ... to call into the public service a large body of volunteers to serve for not less than six or twelve months unless sooner discharged....

Although Great Britain and the United States were able to settle their claims to Oregon amicably, President Polk signed a declaration of war against Mexico on May 13, 1846.

The war was an uneven match from the start. A U.S. force under John Frémont was sent to California to defend the settlers who had declared their independence from Mexico. Colonel Stephen Kearny led U.S. troops into what is today New Mexico, where they captured Santa Fe. The main U.S. force, under General Zachary Taylor, defeated the Mexican army at the Rio Grande and marched southward, where they captured the Mexican city of Monterrey. A U.S. naval force took the port of Tampico on the Gulf of Mexico. Still the Mexicans refused to surrender.

President Polk and General Winfield Scott, commander of all U.S. forces, decided to strike at the heart of the country. In March 1847, a large contingent of marines landed at Veracruz. After six months of fighting, in which four thousand Mexicans and one thousand Americans died, the marines captured Mexico City. The Treaty of Guadalupe Hidalgo, signed on February 2, 1848, set forth the new territories that Mexico ceded to the United States.

TREATY OF GUADALUPE HIDALGO: 1848

… The boundary line between the two Republics shall commence in the Gulf of Mexico … opposite the mouth of the Rio Grande … from thence up the middle of that river, following its deepest channel … to the point where it strikes the southern boundary of New Mexico; thence, westwardly, along the whole southern boundary of New Mexico … until it intersects with the river Gila … thence across the Rio Colorado, following the division line between Upper and Lower California, to the Pacific Ocean.…

Immediately after the treaty shall have been duly ratified … the sum of three millions of dollars shall be paid … by … the United States … in the gold or silver coin of Mexico. The remaining twelve millions of dollars shall be paid … in the same coin, in annual installments of three millions of dollars each.…

GOLD IS DISCOVERED IN CALIFORNIA

In the winter of 1848, James W. Marshall, a millwright, was building a sawmill for John Sutter, a German-born immigrant, for his ranch in the foothills of California's Sierra Nevada mountains. One morning, when Marshall was inspecting the stream that would provide the water power for the mill, he noticed some bright yellow specks in the water. He had discovered gold!

When news of the discovery finally got out, tens of thousands of people headed west, hoping to make their fortunes. Some came by ship around the tip of South America. Others took steamers to Panama, crossed the isthmus on mules, and then sailed up the Pacific coast. Most, however, made the arduous five-month trip across the country by wagon train.

JAMES MARSHALL'S ACCOUNT OF THE FIRST GOLD DISCOVERY IN CALIFORNIA: 1848

… While we were in the habit at night of turning the water through the tail race … I used to go down in the morning to see what had been done by the water through the night; and about half past seven o'clock on or about the 19th of January … I went down as usual, and after shutting off the water from the race I stepped into it … and there upon the rock, about six inches beneath the surface of the water, I DISCOVERED THE GOLD. I was entirely alone at the time. I picked up one or two pieces and examined them attentively; and having some general knowledge of minerals, I could not call to mind more than two which in any way resembled this—sulphuret of iron, very bright and brittle; and gold, bright, yet malleable;… I then collected four or five pieces and went up to Mr. Scott … with the pieces in my hand and said, "I have found it."

"What is it?" inquired Scott.

"Gold," I answered.…

66 'What is it?' inquired Scott. 'Gold,' I answered. 99

▲ An 1866 photograph of Sutter's Creek, where gold was first discovered, which led to the gold rush in California.

U.S. PATENT OF CHARLES GOODYEAR: 1844

Be it known that I, Charles Goodyear ... have invented ... Improvements in the Manner of Preparing ... India-Rubber, ...

My ... improvement consists in ... combining ... sulphur and white lead with the india-rubber, and ... submitting [it] ... to the action of heat at a regulated temperature ... so [it is] far altered ... as not to become softened by ... solar ray or of artificial heat ... nor ... be ... affected by ... cold....

TECHNOLOGICAL ADVANCEMENTS

Americans made many inventive contributions during the nineteenth century. In 1839, Charles Goodyear developed a process that made natural rubber stronger. Elias Howe invented the sewing machine in 1846. In 1832, Samuel F. B. Morse conceived of an electromagnetic telegraph, and in 1844, he built a line from Baltimore to Washington, D.C. Within ten years, thousands of miles of wire crisscrossed the country, making railroad travel safer and business operations more profitable.

▲ An 1869 engraving showing how the cotton gin was used.

27

CHAPTER 5

The Union Starts to Unravel

1850 – 1861

By 1850, California was ready for statehood, but the question of slavery within the lands acquired in the Mexican War had to be settled first. The government turned to Henry Clay. Amid talk of the Southern states seceding from the Union, Clay presented the Omnibus Bill, which would establish the boundaries of Utah, Texas, and New Mexico. The bill failed, however, because all of the measures had to be voted on as one package. These measures were later rescued by introducing them as separate bills and became known as the Compromise of 1850.

The Texas and New Mexico Act of 1850 established the boundaries of Texas and New Mexico. Texas would enter as a slave state, California as a free state. New Mexico would decide for itself. The Utah Act established Utah as a territory, which would decide for itself regarding slavery. The Fugitive Slave Law put all cases of runaway slaves under federal jurisdiction.

TEXAS AND NEW MEXICO ACT: 1850

… The State of Texas cedes to the United States all her claims to territory exterior to the limits and boundaries [established above]….

The United States, in consideration … will pay the State of Texas the sum of ten millions of dollars in a stock bearing five percent interest….

And be it further enacted, that all that portion of the Territory of the United States … [bounded by] the Colorado River … the Rio Grande … the summit of the Sierra Madre … the boundary lines of the State of California … is hereby erected into a temporary government by the name of the Territory of New Mexico … with or without slavery, as their constitution may prescribe….

Freed Slaves Speak Out

Sojourner Truth was born a slave in 1797 and freed by the state of New York in 1828. She worked to abolish slavery and achieve equal rights for women. In 1851, she addressed the Women's Rights Convention in Akron, Ohio, with a speech entitled "Ain't I a Woman?"

Frederick Douglass was also born into slavery in Maryland in 1818, but he escaped to Massachusetts in 1838. He was a gifted orator, and in 1852 on Independence Day, he delivered an address in Rochester, New York.

Sojourner Truth's Address: 1851

Well, children, where there is so much racket there must be something out of kilter. I think that 'twixt the Negroes of the South and the women at the North, all talking about rights, the white men will be in a fix pretty soon....

Then that little man in black there, he says women can't have as much rights as men, 'cause Christ wasn't a woman. Where did your Christ come from? From God and a woman! Man had nothing to do with Him....

Frederick Douglass's Address: 1852

Fellow citizens.... Are the great principles of political freedom ... embodied in that Declaration of Independence, extended to us?...

What, to the American slave, is your Fourth of July? I answer: a day that reveals to him, more than all other days in the year, the gross injustice and cruelty to which he is the constant victim.... There is not a nation on the earth guilty of practices more shocking and bloody than are the people of the United States....

▲ A painting, c.1893, of Abraham Lincoln showing Sojourner Truth a Bible.

POLITICAL REALIGNMENT

In the presidential election of 1852, the Democrats rejected Millard Fillmore, who had become the president upon the death of Zachary Taylor in 1850, and chose Franklin Pierce of New Hampshire as their candidate. Pierce won over the Whig candidate, General Winfield Scott, marking the end of that party.

The Compromise of 1850 had done nothing about slavery in the large, unorganized territories of the Great Plains, but with California wanting a transcontinental rail route to the East, the issue had to be addressed. Illinois Senator Stephen A. Douglas wrote the Kansas-Nebraska Act, which created two territories—Kansas and Nebraska—and declared the Missouri Compromise null and void.

The new territories would each decide whether to have slavery by a popular vote. Kansas was beset by violence as pro-slavery and anti-slavery settlers tried to gain control of the territorial government.

On October 4, 1854, Douglas came to Springfield, Illinois, to defend the Kansas-Nebraska Act. The next night, Abraham Lincoln, a young lawyer, spoke in opposition to the act and urged all citizens to vote against slavery in their states. He said that the Kansas-Nebraska Act was practically legislating slavery. To Lincoln, slavery was incompatible with American democracy, but he avoided abolitionist doctrine because he felt slavery was a national problem, not merely a Southern one.

LINCOLN'S SPEECH ON THE KANSAS-NEBRASKA ACT: 1854

… It is argued that slavery will not go to Kansas and Nebraska…. I have some hope that it will not; but let us not be too confident….

If there is anything which it is the duty of the whole people to never entrust to any hands but their own, that thing is the preservation and perpetuity, of their own liberties, and institution. And if they shall think, as I do, that the extension of slavery endangers them, more than any, or all other causes, how recreant to themselves, if they submit the question, and with it, the fate of their country, to a mere hand-full of men….

James Buchanan, the Democratic candidate, won the presidential election of 1856. On March 6, 1857, the Supreme Court handed down its decision in *Dred Scott* v. *Sanford*. As a slave, Scott had been taken by his master from the slave state of Missouri to the free state of Illinois and then to the free territory of Wisconsin, in the 1830s.

When his master died, Scott tried unsuccessfully to buy his freedom. He took the matter to court, arguing that although he had been returned to Missouri, his past residence in a free state and a free territory had made him a free person. Chief Justice Roger Taney said that Scott was a slave, not a citizen of the United States, and therefore had no right to bring suit in the federal courts. The newspapers reported the decision, with each one reflecting its own political slant.

NEWSPAPER REPORTS OF THE DRED SCOTT DECISION: 1857

Albany, New York Evening Journal
… It is no novelty to find the Supreme Court following the lead of the Slavery Extension Party, to which most of its members belong.…

Columbus, Wisconsin Republican Journal
… It strikes at the very vitals of our free institutions.…

Cincinnati, Ohio Daily Enquirer
… This is a complete vindication of the doctrine of the [Kansas]-Nebraska Bill.…

Richmond, Virginia Enquirer
… [It is] in repudiation of the diabolical doctrines inculcated by factionists and fanatics; and that too by a tribunal of jurists, as learned, impartial and unprejudiced as perhaps the world has ever seen.…

◀ An 1857 wood engraving of Dred Scott, his wife, and his two children that appeared in a newspaper following the Supreme Court ruling.

LINCOLN-DOUGLAS DEBATES

The campaign for the Illinois Senate seat in 1858 pitted the two-term incumbent, Stephen A. Douglas, against his lesser known challenger, Abraham Lincoln. At the time, Douglas was one of the leading Democratic figures of the day, but his reputation had plummeted after the Kansas-Nebraska Act and the violence that followed it.

Douglas had tried to recover some of his previous standing by attacking President Buchanan's plan to recognize a pro-slavery minority government in Kansas. Lincoln was a successful lawyer and state politician, but he did not have a national reputation. Reluctantly, Douglas agreed to meet him in a series of debates throughout the state.

The question of the extension of slavery into the territories acquired from Mexico dominated the seven debates. In the seventh debate, held in Alton, Illinois, on October 15, 1858, Abraham Lincoln defended his antislavery beliefs. Lincoln lost the election for the senate seat, but because of his impressive speaking, he became a national figure. He was popular in the North but was hated in the South.

LINCOLN'S SEVENTH DEBATE WITH DOUGLAS: 1858

… It is a right established by the Constitution of the United States to take a slave into a territory of the United States and hold him as property.… Now … I pass to consider the real … obligation.… Let me take the gentleman [Douglas] who looks me in the face before me, and let us suppose that he is a member of the territorial legislature. The first thing he will do will be to swear that he will support the Constitution of the United States. His neighbor … in the territory has slaves and needs territorial legislation to enable him to enjoy that constitutional right. Can he withhold the legislation which his neighbor needs … which he has sworn to support?… I do not believe it is a constitutional right to hold slaves.… I believe the decision was improperly made, and I go for reversing it. Judge Douglas is furious against those who go for reversing a decision. But he is for legislating it out of all force while the law itself stands.…

THE RAID ON HARPERS FERRY

By October 16, 1859, the fanatical abolitionist John Brown, who had already murdered slave owners in Kansas and Missouri, had raided the United States armory at Harpers Ferry, Virginia (now West Virginia). Brown and four others were captured and put on trial. On November 2, 1859, he spoke before the court in Charlestown and expressed the reasons for his actions.

Many Northerners hailed Brown as a martyr. Southerners believed that Brown had connections with prominent abolitionists and that his raid was part of a wider conspiracy to mobilize slaves in a mass insurrection.

JOHN BROWN'S SPEECH BEFORE THE COURT: 1859

... I have always freely admitted [what] I had done ... in behalf of His despised poor.... Now if it is deemed necessary that I should forfeit my life for the furtherance of the ends of justice, and mingle my blood further with the blood of my children and with the blood of millions in this slave country whose rights are disregarded by wicked, cruel, and unjust enactments—I say, let it be done....

◀ An 1859 wood engraving depicts insurgents being fired upon at Harpers Ferry.

THE BREAKUP OF THE UNION

To many people, the Republican Party was the party of the abolitionists, so to counter that image, the delegates broadened their platform for the election of 1860 to include a protective tariff, free homesteads from the public domain, and a more moderate stand on slavery. The delegates chose Abraham Lincoln as their candidate, because he was less radical than William Seward, long known for his abolitionist views.

The Democrats also faced the challenge of choosing a candidate who would appeal to all factions of their party. Stephen A. Douglas wanted the party's nomination, but he had alienated Southern Democrats by not supporting slavery in the territories, and they moved to block his nomination. When Douglas managed to obtain a majority for his version of the platform, the delegates from eight of the Southern states walked out of the convention. All compromise efforts failed, and the Democrats ended up with two nominees: Douglas for the Northern wing of the party and Vice President John C. Breckinridge of Kentucky for the Southern wing. In effect, this guaranteed Lincoln's victory, but it also signaled to the South that the time had come to secede from the Union.

Secessionists believed that Lincoln's election threatened not only their slave property but also their freedom from a coercive government in Washington. They felt that the Republicans were bent on destroying their way of life.

On December 20, 1860, South Carolina passed the Ordinance of Secession, which argued that the Northern states had violated the "constitutional compact" regarding slavery and were thus to blame for the breakup of the Union.

Following South Carolina's lead, Mississippi, Florida, Alabama, Georgia, Louisiana, and Texas all seceded from the Union.

SOUTH CAROLINA'S ORDINANCE OF SECESSION: 1860

... We, the people of the State of South Carolina, in Convention assembled, do declare and ordain ... that the union now subsisting between South Carolina and other States under the name of the United States of America is hereby dissolved....

CONSTITUTION OF THE CONFEDERATE STATES: 1861

We, the people of the Confederate States, each State acting in its sovereign and independent character ... do ordain and establish this Constitution for the Confederate States of America....

Article I, Section IX

... The importation of negroes of the African race from any foreign country other than the slaveholding States or Territories of the United States of America, is hereby forbidden; and Congress is required to pass such laws as shall effectually prevent the same....

Article IV, Section II

... The citizens of each State shall be entitled to all the privileges and immunities of citizens in several States; and shall have the right of transit and sojourn in any State of this Confederacy, with their slaves and other property, and the right of property in said slaves shall not be thereby impaired....

❝... do ordain and establish this Constitution for the Confederate States of America....❞

In February 1861, before Lincoln could take the presidential oath of office, representatives from the seven secessionist states met in Alabama to draft a constitution for their new country—the Confederate States of America. Jefferson Davis, a former senator from Mississippi, was elected president of the Confederacy.

For some Southerners, leaving the Union posed new and troubling issues, but these problems were not strong enough to prevent secession.

▲ An undated print of Jefferson Davis and the cabinet of the new Confederate States of America.

35

CHAPTER 6

The Civil War

1861–1865

Although it seemed hopeless, Senator John Crittenden of Kentucky made a last-minute effort to find a compromise to stop the breakup of the Union. The critical issue now was no longer slavery but whether the Southern states would be allowed to secede.

By the time Abraham Lincoln took office in Washington, D.C., the Confederacy had commandeered all government buildings and most military installations and arsenals within its territory. A civil war was now inevitable. In Lincoln's first inaugural address on March 4, 1861, he pleaded for peace and recalled how the patriots had fought to gain independence and to form this Union.

THE WAR BEGINS

Fort Sumter, located on an island in the harbor of Charleston, South Carolina, was still in the hands of the United States, but by April 12, 1861, the South could no longer abide a continued Union presence there. Confederate artillery opened fire, and the United States forces surrendered. Lincoln called for seventy-five thousand volunteers to suppress the insurrection. The Civil War had begun.

LINCOLN'S FIRST INAUGURAL ADDRESS: 1861

… I am loath to close. We are not enemies, but friends. We must not be enemies. Though passion may have strained, it must not break our bonds of affection. The mystic chords of memory, stretching from every battlefield, and patriot grave, to every living heart and hearthstone, all over this broad land, will yet swell the chorus of the Union, when again touched, as surely they will be, by the better angels of our nature.…

◄ An 1864 drawing of Fort Sumter, after it had surrendered to the Confederates. The attack on Fort Sumter marked the start of the Civil War.

Within the next month, Virginia, North Carolina, Arkansas, and Tennessee joined the Confederacy. After the first battles in the East, the Union's hope for a quick victory faded. The Anaconda Plan was drawn up by Union general-in-chief Winfield Scott, who presented it to Major General George B. McClellan, to carry out. Named for a type of boa constrictor, the plan was intended to crush the South between a naval blockade of the Atlantic and Gulf coasts and an invasion along the Mississippi, Cumberland, and Tennessee Rivers.

THE ANACONDA PLAN: 1861

Maj. Gen. George B. McClellan, Commanding Ohio Volunteers:...

Sir:

... It is the design of the Government to raise 25,000 additional regular troops, and 60,000 volunteers for three years....

We rely greatly on ... a complete blockage of the Atlantic and Gulf ports soon to commence. In connection with such blockade we propose a powerful movement down the Mississippi to the ocean.... Finally, it will be necessary that New Orleans should be strongly occupied and securely held....

FROM BULL RUN TO ANTIETAM

In October 1861, Union forces were defeated at the Battle of Ball's Bluff in Virginia, and Lincoln replaced General Scott with General McClellan. Union forces narrowly prevailed at the Battle of Shiloh in April 1862, but losses on both sides were heavy.

In August 1862, Stonewall Jackson and his Confederate forces defeated the Union troops at the Battle of Cedar Mountain in Virginia. At the Second Battle of Bull Run in Manassas, Virginia, in August 1862, the combined forces of Robert E. Lee, Stonewall Jackson, and James Longstreet pushed the Union troops back to Washington, D.C. At the Battle of Antietam in Maryland in September 1862, General McClellan forced Lee to retreat from previously won forward positions. On October 25, 1862, a Union soldier wrote a letter to a friend, describing the battlefield conditions and his longing for home.

▲ An 1862 photograph of a New York infantry company at Manassas at the Second Battle of Bull Run.

LETTER FROM A UNION SOLDIER TO A DEAR FRIEND: 1862

Dear Miss

I will Inform you that I am well at this time…. I was Glad to Hear from you & that you was well…. I do love to get News from Home for it looks as if that is all the consolation that us Soldiers Have … & We Have to do as Best we can….

My Self & H. W. Reitzel & J. M. Osborn will Be on guard Sunday &

Sunday night I hope that we will leave for a warmer climate Soon.... I would Inform you that one of Capt Nobles men Died last night His name is Taylor.... Indeed Dear Miss there is thousands of Poor Soldiers that will see Home & Friends no more in this World If you [could] ... See the number of Sick & Disabled Soldiers it would make your Heart Ache. They are Dying ... Every Day.... But don't think that I am Home Sick or Disheartened for such is not the case for I am only telling you a few simple Facts of a Soldiers campaign Indeed I wish never to Return Home Permanently until this Wicked & God Forsaken Rebellion is Destroyed—If we had our choices ... we would Be at Home for we are not in the army for fun nor money & ... we wish never to fill a cowards grave.... Success to the union Armys & Ere Long may we all Be permitted to Return to our Homes & Live a quiet & Peaceable Lives.

... Please write Soon & tell all to ... write to the Soldiers for it gives them great Pleasure to hear from Home....

◀ An 1861 photograph of two Union soldiers.

THE EMANCIPATION PROCLAMATION

Despite Lincoln's plan for gradual emancipation, he soon realized he had to take immediate action. Slaves were an asset to the Confederate war effort, and Northerners were starting to favor emancipation. On September 22, 1862, he issued a proclamation declaring that all slaves within Confederate States were to be set free.

THE EMANCIPATION PROCLAMATION: 1862

... On the 1st day of January, A.D. 1863, all persons held as slaves within any States ... the people whereof shall then be in rebellion against the United States shall be then, thenceforward, and forever free....

GETTYSBURG AND VICKSBURG

General Lee realized that the Confederacy's only hope of victory was to bring the war to the North. On July 1, 1863, the Army of Northern Virginia confronted the Union forces at Gettysburg, Pennsylvania. The South suffered its worst defeat. At the same time, Confederate troops under siege at Vicksburg, Mississippi, surrendered, giving the Union complete control of the Mississippi River.

▲ A lithograph, c.1863, depicts the Battle of Gettysburg, which was a pivotal victory for the Union.

The battles of Gettysburg and Vicksburg were turning points for the Union cause. On November 19, 1863, President Lincoln delivered an address at a dedication ceremony for a cemetery at Gettysburg.

THE GETTYSBURG ADDRESS: 1863

Four score and seven years ago our fathers brought forth on this continent, a new nation, conceived in Liberty, and dedicated to the proposition that all men are created equal.

Now we are engaged in a great civil war, testing whether that nation, or any nation so conceived and so dedicated, can long endure. We are met on a great battlefield of that war. We have come to dedicate a portion of that field, as a final resting place for those who here gave their lives that that nation might live. It is altogether fitting and proper that we should do this.

But, in a larger sense, we can not dedicate—we can not consecrate—we can not hallow—this ground. The brave men, living and dead, who struggled here, have consecrated it, far above our poor power to add or detract. The world will little note, nor long remember what we say here, but it can never forget what they did here. It is for us the living, rather, to be dedicated here to the unfinished work which they who fought here have thus far so nobly advanced. It is rather for us to be here dedicated to the great task remaining before us—that from these honored dead we take increased devotion to that cause for which they gave the last full measure of devotion—that we here highly resolve that these dead shall not have died in vain—that this nation, under God, shall have a new birth of freedom—and that government of the people, by the people, for the people, shall not perish from the earth.

In March 1864, President Lincoln named Ulysses S. Grant as commander of all Union forces. In May, Grant ordered General William T. Sherman to burn Atlanta, Georgia. Sherman captured Savannah and then moved on to South Carolina.

On December 25, 1862, a Confederate soldier, Tally Simpson, wrote a letter to his sister, describing the destruction he saw at Fredricksburg, Virginia.

TALLY SIMPSON'S LETTER: 1862

My dear sister,

... If all the dead ... could be heaped in one pile and all the wounded be gathered ... the pale faces of the dead and the groans of the wounded would send ... a thrill of horror through the hearts of the originators of this war....

I have often read of ... pillaged towns in ancient history, but never, till I saw Fredricksburg, did I fully realize what one was. The houses ... are riddled with shell and ball. The stores have been broken open and deprived of every thing that was worth a shilling. Account books ... letters and papers ... were ... scattered ... and trampled under feet. Private property was ruined. Their soldiers [Union] would sleep in the mansions ... and use the articles and food ... at their pleasure.... Such a wreck and ruin I never wish to see again....

LINCOLN'S REELECTION

In the election of 1864, the Republicans nominated Lincoln for a second term. The party's platform called for the Confederacy's unconditional surrender and a constitutional amendment abolishing slavery. The Democrats chose General George McClellan as their candidate. They attacked Lincoln's handling of the war, criticized emancipation, and urged an immediate armistice. As casualties mounted, public support for the war was uncertain, but victories in the South—especially the fall of Atlanta—boosted the president's campaign, and he was reelected.

LINCOLN'S SECOND INAUGURAL ADDRESS: 1865

... With malice toward none, with charity for all, with firmness in the right as God gives us to see the right, let us strive on to finish the work we are in, to bind up the nation's wounds, to care for him who shall have borne the battle and for his widow and his orphan, to do all which may achieve and cherish a just and lasting peace among ourselves and with all nations.

THE END OF THE WAR

When General Grant captured an important railroad junction near Richmond, Virginia, the Confederate capital, General Robert E. Lee and his army were trapped. Lee sent messengers to Grant announcing that he was ready to surrender. On April 9, 1865, the two generals met at Appomattox, Virginia, marking the end of the war.

A lithograph, c.1865, depicting the surrender of General Lee to General Grant. ▶

GENERAL LEE'S SURRENDER AT APPOMATTOX: 1865

[General Grant]: I received your letter of this date containing the terms of the surrender of the army of Northern Virginia, as proposed by you. As they are substantially the same as those expressed in your letter of the 8th instant, they are accepted. I will proceed to designate the proper officers to carry the stipulations into effect.

R. E. Lee, General

LINCOLN'S ASSASSINATION

With Lee's surrender, the Union had been preserved, yet Lincoln would not live to oversee the reconstruction of the nation. On the evening of April 14, 1865, at Ford's Theater in Washington, D.C., John Wilkes Booth, an actor who was an embittered Southern sympathizer, shot the president in the head. Lincoln died the next day. Twelve days later, troops tracked down and killed Booth.

Millions of Americans publically mourned the president along the route of the funeral train that took his body back to Illinois. People were glad that the war was over, but Lincoln's assassination filled them with a renewed sense of loss and an anxiety about the future.

◀ An undated print depicts John Wilkes Booth assassinating President Lincoln at Ford's Theater in Washington, D.C.

TIME LINE

1816	■ James Monroe is elected the fifth U.S. president.
1820	■ Missouri Compromise preserves the balance of free and slave states.
1823	■ The Monroe Doctrine establishes principles of U.S. foreign policy.
1828	■ Andrew Jackson is elected the seventh U.S. president.
1836	■ Texas wins its independence from Mexico.
1840	■ William Henry Harrison is elected the ninth U.S. president.
1841	■ President Harrison dies and is succeeded by Vice President John Tyler, who becomes the tenth U.S. president.
1845	■ James Polk is elected the eleventh U.S. president.
1845	■ The United States annexes Texas.
1845	■ Manifest Destiny encourages westward expansion.
1846–1848	■ The United States wins new territories after war with Mexico.
1848	■ Gold is discovered in California, sparking a gold rush.
1850	■ President Zachary Taylor dies and is succeeded by Vice President Millard Fillmore, who becomes the thirteenth U.S. president.
1852	■ Franklin Pierce is elected the fourteenth U.S. president.
1857	■ The Supreme Court decision of *Dred Scott* v. *Sanford* declares that Congress cannot ban slavery and that slaves are not citizens.
1859	■ Abolitionist John Brown leads raid at Harpers Ferry.
1860	■ Abraham Lincoln is elected the sixteenth U.S. president.
1860–1861	■ Eleven Southern states secede from the Union.
1861	■ The Confederate States of America is established.
1861–1865	■ The Northern and Southern states fight the Civil War.
1863	■ The Emancipation Proclamation declares slaves free.
1865	■ General Lee surrenders to General Grant, ending the Civil War.
1865	■ Lincoln is assassinated by John Wilkes Booth.

GLOSSARY

abolitionists: people who wants to do away with slavery.

annexation: act of adding or joining to, as one country to another.

assimilated: to make something a part of something else.

ceding: surrendering possession of something.

chief justice: presiding judge of the Supreme Court.

commandeered: forcibly took over for military use.

compromise: settlement of differences.

Confederacy: union of Southern states in opposition to the Union.

creditor: person or business to whom money is owed.

delegates: persons authorized to represent other people.

emancipation: freedom from oppression.

expansionist: person who wants to increase the size of a country by adding new territory.

federal government: union of states that recognizes a strong central government.

force bill: law that makes people or states do something they might not otherwise want to do.

inaugural address: speech a president gives after he is elected.

Manifest Destiny: belief that the U.S. government had the right to settle the continent from coast to coast.

millwright: person who repairs mills or mill machinery.

Monroe Doctrine: U.S. policy of opposition to outside interference in the Americas.

nationalism: devotion to the interests of a particular country.

nullify: to do away with something.

perpetuity: forever.

platform: declaration of the principles on which a person or a political party appeals to the public.

political alignment: grouping of people or countries with similar political beliefs.

repudiate: to reject.

secede: to withdraw from something, such as a state from a country.

sectionalism: excessive devotion to local interests.

Supreme Court: highest court in the United States.

tariffs: taxes imposed by a government on imported good.

veto: to reject a bill passed by the law-making body of a government.

Whigs: American political party that favored high tariffs and a loose interpretation of the Constitution.

FURTHER INFORMATION

BOOKS

Bolotin, Norman. *The Civil War A to Z: A Young Readers' Guide to over 100 People, Places, and Points of Importance.* Dutton Children's Books/Penguin Putnam, 2002.

McPherson, James M. *Fields of Fury: the American Civil War.* Atheneum Books for Young Readers, 2002.

Stanley, George E. *Andrew Jackson—Young Patriot,* Childhood of Famous Americans. Simon & Schuster/Aladdin Books, 2003.

WEB SITES

statelibrary.dcr.state.nc.us/nc/bio/public/Jackson.htm This state of North Carolina Web site provides an in-depth look at the life of Andrew Jackson.

www.sunsite.utk.edu/civil-war/ This University Texas Web site provides numerous links to informational resources on many aspects of the Civil War, including "Histories and Bibliographies," "Battles & Campaigns," "Rosters & Regimental Histories," and much more.

USEFUL ADDRESSES

Gettysburg National Military Park
97 Taneytown Road
Gettysburg, PA 17325-2804
Telephone: (717) 334-1124

National Portrait Gallery, Smithsonian Institution
P.O. Box 37012
Victor Building–Suite 8300 MRC 973
Washington, DC 20013-7012
Telephone: (202) 275-1738

★ ★ ★ INDEX ★ ★ ★